How to Teach Driving
Behind the Wheel, Lesson by Lesson
Instructors' Edition

How to Teach Driving

Behind the Wheel, Lesson by Lesson

Instructors' Edition

Kenneth Lindquist

Fresh Ink Group
Guntersville

How to Teach Driving
Behind the Wheel, Lesson-by-Lesson
Instructors' Edition

Fresh Ink Group
An Imprint of:
The Fresh Ink Group, LLC
1021 Blount Avenue #931
Guntersville, AL 35976
Email: info@FreshInkGroup.com
FreshInkGroup.com

Edition 1.0   2022

Cover design by Stephen Geez / FIG
Book design by Amit Dey / FIG
Associate publisher Lauren A. Smith / FIG

Cataloging-in-Publication Recommendations:
TRA001080   TRANSPORTATION / Automotive / Driver Education
EDU029090.   EDUCATION / Teaching / Materials & Devices
EDU029100.   EDUCATION / Teaching / Methods & Strategies

Library of Congress Control Number: 2022905039

ISBN-13: 978-1-947893-45-0 Papercover
ISBN-13: 978-1-947893-46-7 Hardcover
ISBN-13: 978-1-947893-47-4 Ebooks

Table of Contents

Foreword to the Teacher

Other driving manuals analyze vehicles and driving by breaking down the details and functions. It is useful information, but analysis doesn't explain how it all comes together and that is what the beginning driver needs to know. That synthesis has to come from the teacher in the real world.

This book focuses on the sequences of teaching to drive and is the answer to the question of, "What do I, the teacher, do or say next?" It's intended to be a manual for commercial driving school instructors or public school instructors.

Before you, the teacher, begin to think too deeply about teaching driving, you'll feel that your years of driving experience will be enough. Then you get into the vehicle with the student or students and you find you're not certain what to bring up first. It's an important day for the students and the teacher and there needs to be a plan.

I recommend you read through the book quickly to be familiar with what is covered and the timing of the skills and the overall plan. Then later follow the chapters in order except for the chapters on problem areas and night driving. The problem area chapter is meant to summarize problems and their solutions and be a quick reference if needed. The section on problem areas and their remedies will shorten the time needed to build skills, and the additional advice on specialized driving situations will bring up new topics to discuss with the student. The chapter on night driving can be used any time after the chapter on driving on two-lane roads.

Wording in this book that covers the full width of the page is intended generally to direct the teacher to do something. The teacher can skip from action to action while in the vehicle, if that is what the situation demands, and find it easier to keep track of the section being covered.

The indented lines contain explanations for the actions, further information, and notes.

Preliminary

An experienced driver handles a vehicle without conscious thought to the intricate factors involved. That's why it is difficult to teach a beginner who needs to know the individual motions. The experienced driver will have to deconstruct how s/he manages, for instance, to take a turn to a side road from a speedy 4-lane. This text will aid in reminding the teacher how things are done, detail by detail, and helping put it into words the beginner will understand.

A student who has ridden a bicycle, a toy car, a go-cart, or a golf cart will have an advantage in learning to drive because of having been in charge of a vehicle. Those experiences condition the student to adjusting steering rate to vehicle speed, understanding the differences in braking results depending on speed, knowing that the back wheels don't follow the same path as the front wheels, and knowing which way to turn when backing or repositioning the vehicle. Those early learning episodes make it much easier to understand the dynamics of the vehicle they are learning on.

Learning can also take place by listening, watching and imitating, if the student is interested. The teacher can explain his/her reading of traffic and driving strategies when the teacher is the one who is driving. The point would be to tell the student what the teacher's driving decisions are when changing speeds, changing lanes, moving from one side of a lane to the other, etc. It should be as if the teacher had thought bubbles showing around them like a cartoon character. That way the student learns that driving requires thinking and judgment.

The teacher's attitude should show that the teacher wants the student to be a competent driver. That is different from not hurting someone else, not harming oneself, and not damaging the car. The teacher's attitude will show up when mistakes are made. All beginners make mistakes so when they happen, saying "I told you so." is not the optimal thing to say. Something more positive, analytic or helpful along the lines of saying "The reason that happened was you started the turn when the car was too close to the curb." Then, at the next turning occasion but <u>in</u> <u>advance</u>, offer the solution, "Stay in the middle of the lane to start the turn."

Response to verbal instructions is slower than response to visual signals so the instructor will need to develop a feel for how much lead time to build into giving instructions and into preventing an error. If the teacher starts a reminder at the same time that the student is taking the right action, the teacher should acknowledge that the student was already doing the right thing.

The student's attitude is helped if the teacher demonstrates competence beyond what the student sees in ordinary daily driving. The easiest skill to show would be an emergency stop engaging ABS (anti-lock braking system). Once the student finds out the teacher can teach actions beyond the usual, the student will be more accepting of what is taught.

An adult student will have watched driving from a responsible viewpoint and will be ready to act as a competent driver because of seeing other adults manage the driving task. However, young student drivers have been impressed by electronic games, CGI scenes in movies and TV stunts. They may also model their driving based on a parent's or a friend's driving habits and "style," or the driving of a bus driver, if that is their model of a good driver. It will be necessary to directly counter the mistaken ideas they have about steering, traction, braking distances, and behavior on the roads.

Getting a learner's license generally requires passing a test of the driving rules and signs. If the reference book or manual is also available online, the young student is more likely to study the online tests than the entire manual. The student thinks it is only a test. We experienced drivers know that our driving knowledge is tested every day on everything in the driver's manual and beyond. Therefore, you might need to require the student to study the manual and pass a test of your questions from time to time.

Once the driving practice begins, it should be scheduled and the schedule kept. Scheduling shows that it is important and it prevents letting too much time elapse between lessons. Beginners need to learn something new, forget it, and then relearn it and practice it to have a new skill become part of them. That technique is called "distributed practice." Once per week is fine at the beginning, then more frequent when the skills are better and more automatic for the student.

Maintaining a once per week schedule is fine too.

Cautions

Develop the habit of telling the student to put the gear shift lever in "park" any time you plan to get out of the vehicle or are about to give lengthy instruction.

Make sure you can see at least one turn signal light on the dashboard from your seat and always double check to see that the correct signal is being made.

Make sure you can see the speedometer or put the speed screen where you can see it without straining.

Don't turn your cell phone off in the car. Show the student that a phone does not need to be answered. Let your phone ring.

Check your vehicle Owner's Manual for warnings about the limitations of the electronic aids. Many will have language stating they are driving aids and should not be solely relied upon. The Manual may say that the lane change warning systems, for instance, may not be effective at less than 20 mph, when there is a large speed differential between vehicles, or a where there is a wide angle to the main traffic flow. Those situations occur in parking lots and at yield signs. Another instance of a driving aid caution may be the automatic emergency braking (AEB) in your vehicle. It may rely on the brake lights of the vehicle ahead but not activate for other objects.

Chapter One

·· + ◆ + ··

Beginner's First Lessons

The student will develop with more confidence if taught the basics of car handling before driving on the road. At later stages it is likewise advisable to teach new skills in a parking lot before having to use the skills in traffic.

This first section has a divided start. One route (A) is a student experiencing his/her first time behind the wheel. The other route (B, page 22) teaches a student who has some driving experience. Some of the material is duplicated for the teacher's convenience.

(A) First time behind the wheel

If the student has (1) never been behind the wheel and has (2) never taken a classroom course, the student has nothing to unlearn and will be very excited.

Driving position

Have the student get into the driver's seat while you are outside the car with the driver's door open. Show the student the seat adjustment controls and guide the student into proper positioning.   The ideal seating position will have the student's eyes about half-way up the windshield. If the student isn't tall enough, a seat cushion is called for. The student's breastbone should be at least 10 inches back from the airbag in the steering wheel. The student should be close enough to the pedals to be able to comfortably press the brake as hard as possible with the right foot without shifting in the seat. Then adjust the steering wheel so the student's elbow bend is 90 to 120 degrees and at a comfortable height when holding the steering wheel with the hands at the 10 and 2 positions as on a clock face. The back of the head should not be touching the head restraint. The seat belt must go over the shoulder to be effective.

Explanation

The airbag deploys at 200 mph for 10 inches to protect the head and face and then deflates. It's difficult to estimate what 10 inches looks like so use this solution: spread your fingers as far apart as possible and measure the distance between the outside of the thumb to the outside of the pinky. You'll likely find it to be 7 or 8 inches. Compare your finger spread to the student's and then the student will have a portable measurement standard.

Right foot braking is recommended. In an emergency, the driver who uses left foot braking is likely to press the brake with the left foot and the gas with the right foot with unfortunate results. The heel of the right foot should remain on the floor for ordinary driving. The foot can then flex left and right between the brake pedal and the gas pedal and control of both pedals is managed with the calf muscles of the leg, not the thigh muscles. This means that high heeled shoes should not be worn on the right foot when driving. Whatever style of shoe is worn on the right foot, it should have a strap or heel surround of some type. That strap/surround will keep the shoe on the foot when moving rapidly between gas and brake in an emergency.

Auto companies design the steering wheels with spokes at what would be the 9 and 3 positions on a clock face and thickened areas above the 10 and 2 positions, thus giving the 10 and 2 positions space to grip the wheel more securely when grip is needed and a place to rest the thumbs. The hands should always remain on the outside of the steering wheel. The 9 and 3 position on the steering wheel is ok but not as good as the 10 and 2. Both positions allow a quick half turn of the wheel with one motion. Signal switches and wiper controls can be activated from the 10 and 2 positions without moving the hands. If the arms are held out too straight in front of the student (beyond 120 degrees), the student will develop pain in the upper shoulder area when driving for long periods.

The head should not be touching the head restraint because when the head is resting on the head restraint, head-turning motions are restricted and the vibrations in the car jiggle the eyes. Some hairstyles just don't work for driving normal vehicles.

Ponytails positioned on the back of the head contact the head restraint and are a constant annoyance, and tall hair styles can rub on the roof of the vehicle, making the student a bit claustrophobic. Hair styles that frame the face often block peripheral vision so there needs to be a way to keep the hair back while driving. Tucking the hair behind the ears doesn't work long enough.

Some students may try to wear just the lap portion of the seat belt which, of course, is not adequate. The instructor must insist on wearing the seat belt properly in the beginning. An exercise provided later will be the convincing argument.

Left and right

You may be surprised to find that students confuse left and right. It happens more often with people for whom English is not their native language. Luckily there is a reminder in the car. The outside mirror adjustment mechanisms on the door or on the dashboard are labeled "L" and "R" in the correct relative positions and are a good reminder to the students every time they enter the car.

Starting the vehicle

From inside the vehicle, show the student how to start it.

Explanation

If the vehicle starts with a key, it's possible that the steering wheel lock will engage and not allow the key to turn. This is a good time to explain the steering wheel lock's purpose (anti-theft and prevent accidentally rolling into traffic when parked) and how to wiggle the steering wheel while turning the key to get the engine started. It's also a good time to explain that a key ring loaded with keys and souvenirs can accidently be brushed by the knee in a way that turns the engine off and locks the steering wheel while the car is still moving. It too produces an unfortunate result.

Show the student that the tachometer (on the dashboard) measures the speed of the engine's turning.

Explanation

When a warmed gasoline engine is running at idle, the tachometer will show the engine is turning about 750 revolutions per minute. Some gasoline powered vehicles are very quiet, and it is difficult to hear the engine at idle. In such a case, the student who doesn't look at the tachometer may attempt to start the engine when it is already running. Modern cars equipped with electronics will not let the starter engage the engine while it is running, but vintage cars may let the driver operate the starter. When both the engine and the starter mesh and turn but at different rates, the teeth on the starter's gears will be ground away in a very noisy manner.

Steering practice

Before making the car move, it's a good idea to practice steering motions.

Explanation

The experienced driver may think the beginner has been alert to steering and braking, watched others perform those actions, and knows what to do and when to do it. That is a wrong assumption.

Have the student grip the wheel with the hands at about the 10 o'clock and 2 o'clock positions using enough force to turn the wheel but not tightly clenched. Then swing the wheel back and forth using both hands. That action provides as much as a half turn of the steering wheel with one motion.   It is used in normal driving on curving roads and is the start of any turn to a new road. To make the sharper turn to a new road generally requires a half turn of the wheel followed by a quarter turn of the wheel. To make a 90-degree right turn, the student should turn the wheel to the right using both hands. As the left hand approaches the 3 or 4 o'clock position (and continues), the right hand comes off the wheel and moves to the 12 o'clock position of the continuously moving wheel and pulls the wheel down to about the 3 or 4 o'clock position. As soon as the right hand grips the wheel at 12 o'clock, the left hand releases the wheel and stays ready to either grasp the wheel at 12 o'clock to further the turn, or to grasp the wheel at 10 o'clock after the right hand returns the wheel to the starting position at the conclusion of the turn. The same motion is used for a turn to the left but with the opposite hands.

The hand-over-hand technique described in steps above is the fastest way to turn the wheel in an emergency maneuver so it should be the main method of steering and the first one learned. It should be the "go to" method. The hands should remain on the outside of the steering wheel. It will be easier to demonstrate the wheel turning than to describe it well enough that the student gets it.

A different form of steering, one which keeps the hands from crossing the center of the steering wheel, was developed to avoid the driver being scuffed when the steering wheel airbag explodes while turning. This method of steering requires that a vehicle making a turn be driven at an unusually slow speed if the turning vehicle is to stay within the new lane. That happens because the wheel is being turned in 3 quarter-turn increments, which is a very slow process. The faster steering that can come from the hand-over-hand motion is more likely to avoid the wreck and thereby prevent a scuffing event.

Braking practice

Before making the car move, it's a good idea to practice braking motions.

Explanation

The student's heel should be on the floor for ordinary brake and gas control. Using the calf muscles to apply pressure gives better control. Sometimes the student doesn't know which pedal is which. To help the student better understand that vehicles are logically designed, point out that the gas pedal is located directly ahead of the right leg where it can comfortably stay for hours at a time. The brake pedal is used much less and so is centered. Have the student practice the motion of going back and forth between the gas pedal and brake pedal and applying each. There is a place on the left side of the driver's footwell for the left foot to rest or to provide body balance when turning right. The clutch pedal (of a manually shifted vehicle) is located directly in front of the left leg. The clutch is used more frequently than the brake but for shorter periods.

Moving the Vehicle

Direct the student to put the right foot on the brake, push the shift release button (if there is one) and put the gear selector into the "drive" position.

Explanation

The brake must be engaged to move the gear selector out of "park" but the gear selector can then be moved to any and all positions.

Ask the student to look in all directions to check if it is safe to move the vehicle, then tell the student to take the foot off the brake and apply the gas pedal lightly, using the calf muscles. Let the student drive at a modest pace.

> The student will be too excited to keep watch for safety so that task is up to the teacher. Let the student choose the speed unless it becomes dangerous.

Have the student steer left and right (swerving) while keeping both hands on the steering wheel, in other words no hand-over-hand steering at first.

Tell the student to stop at the end of the parking lot on the first pass, then tell the student to use hand-over-hand steering to turn the car 180 degrees and aim at the starting point, then stop.

Explanation

> When the student over steers, explain that most passenger vehicle's steering will cover the full range of steering motion in three full turns of the wheel (3 turns lock-to-lock or, in other words, one and a half turns from straight ahead to the end of the steering motion in either direction). Show the student what the steering wheel appearance is when the wheel is straight and when it is one complete turn in either direction. Tell the student to let the vehicle roll forward an inch or two to determine if the steering is aimed straight or if it is in a turning position. Adjust accordingly and complete the pass to the starting point.

Repeat passes back and forth a few times. Then add an explanation of how to make a gentle stop.

Explanation

> A gentle stop can be reached by slowing almost to a stop then easing the foot pressure off the brake so that the full stop comes while moving 1 or 2 mph instead of from 10 mph.

Next, add slowing and turning instead of stopping to make new passes. If there are islands, other vehicles or other features in the parking lot, work up to going around them. The student may change steering motions when making actual turns rather than the steering practice. This is when you may see the student start a turn by putting the hand into the steering wheel instead of keeping it on the outside of the wheel.

Steering problem

> Putting the hand inside the steering wheel, palm up, while turning.

Solution

> Remind the student to keep the hands on the outside of the steering wheel. There are three reasons to do so: 3. The palm up hand position is very restrictive, allowing only about a quarter turn of the wheel; 2. The forearm is situated over the air bag with the fingers looped around the wheel, potentially causing a very painful extension of the fingers if the air bag explodes; 1. <u>The most important reason is the driver's</u>

<u>eyes are looking inside the vehicle to avoid hitting the steering wheel spokes with the hand while the driver is turning.</u>

This is the time to explain to the student that drivers tend to drive in the direction they are looking.

Explanation

The driver needs to look where the driver <u>does</u> want the vehicle to go – not where s/he <u>doesn't</u> want to go. Humans use their eyes for aiming. That's something we know about from sports and games. So, if drivers look at what they don't want to hit (debris, pothole, etc.), they will likely hit what they are looking at. Other common examples: A driver looking to the right to see a phone will steer toward the right, recover and do it again; Drivers steer toward pedestrians and lighted police cars they are looking at intently.

The first lessons are stressful on the student as well as the teacher. If the lesson lasts too long, the student loses concentration and begins to make errors. If that happens, end the lesson for that day. Teachers should expect an hour or so of good attention.

If the student is making progress, add backing to the mix.

Explanation

At the end of a pass, tell the student to stop and put the car into "park". Explain that (1) when going forward, the driver steers in the direction s/he wants the front of the vehicle to go; (2) when backing the driver steers in the direction s/he wants the back to go. Most beginners think it must be harder than that. Check to see that there is plenty of space and tell the driver to put the vehicle into "reverse." Let the student keep the backing speed slow and try steering left and right to confirm that steering in the direction s/he wants the back to go is correct. There are only two directions so if one way is wrong, the other must be correct. For some students, it works to have them look where they want the back of the vehicle to go and then steer in the direction they are looking.

Before ending the first lesson, try urging the student to reach 20 or 25 mph (assuming that is safe in the lot being used). It's a confidence builder.

Explanation

A speed of 20 -25 mph is the speed limit typically found in a neighborhood so having the student reach that speed once or twice in a parking lot means the student knows s/he can handle that speed. The student's self-confidence will grow as well as confidence in the teacher.

Second lesson behind the wheel

The second lesson should begin in a parking lot and, ideally, continue to a subdivision or neighborhood that is nearby. The teacher will need to decide if the student is ready for driving on the roads based on parking lot success.

Instruct the student to practice the steering motions while still parked. The student should first swing the steering wheel back and forth without moving the hands along the wheel. Then practice the hand-over-hand steering for right and left turns.

Explanation

A right turn generally requires a half turn (using both hands) and a quarter turn (where the right hand comes off the wheel, grabs the top of the steering wheel and pulls down to about the 3 o'clock position) to stay within the correct lane. A left turn uses less steering because the vehicle is crossing a lane which means the turn is not as tight as a right turn. If the student takes too much time before the quarter turn, explain that the turn requires the motions to be done "one-two."

Occasionally a student may just not "get" steering. S/he will make what seem to be random motions of the steering wheel for actual turns even though parking lot steering practice was adequate. To accustom the student to the turning motions, direct the student to make figure 8's in a parking lot. Make sure the student turns the steering wheel all the way left and then all the way right in making the 8's. The exercise will help develop the "muscle memory" for turning.

Point out to the student which of the controls on the steering wheel is the signal switch. Instruct the student to operate the switch without looking at it. It is always in the same place. If the student has trouble knowing which way to move the switch, show how the intended turning of the steering wheel is the clue to which way to turn the switch.

For instance, if the switch is on the left side of the steering column, a turn to the left will have the left hand moving down and down is the direction for the signal switch for a left turn. If the switch is on the right side of the steering column, a left turn will have the right hand moving up and up is the direction needed for that switch to show a left turn.

Call the student's attention to the mirrors and explain to the student how they should be adjusted.

Explanation

> The inside mirror should show the entire back window. The outside mirrors should show just a bit of the vehicle in the left-right plane and a long-distance view of the road in the up-down plane. The teacher will find that having the student seated properly means less mirror adjustment when changing seats back and forth with the student. In effect, the driver is adjusted more than the mirrors.

Tell the student to drive in the parking lot but let the student choose the speed at first. Next, have the student practice slowing for turns by using the parking lot features like islands as objects to drive around. The back of a shopping center may be useful.

> This would be a good time to point out the speedometer and how to read it, as well as practice using the turn signals.

At this juncture, the student has practiced all the parts of making a turn and it's time to put it all together.

Practice the complete sequence for a turn. That is "signal, slow, turn, straighten, resume."

> A student will typically return the wheel to the straight-ahead position too soon. The experienced driver waits until the car is aligned to the road ahead before straightening. Another way to phrase the time to straighten is to have the student wait until the vehicle is centered in the lane of the new road.

Encourage the student to reach 20 mph or 25 mph after warm-up driving.

This is an appropriate time to practice emergency braking. The student will make many mistakes, and that is an expectation of the student as well. Practicing what to do in an emergency will give the student confidence that s/he can do the right thing in an emergency and that mistakes are accepted.

Explanation and description—emergency braking

> **Supplies needed** – Two traffic cones for the braking area. Others may be needed if a lane must be marked out to keep the student aligned to the braking area.

Describe Antilock Braking System (ABS) to the student.

> ## *Explanation*
>
> The owner's manual should have a description or use this one. All passenger vehicles built in 2012 and

later must have ABS and it is likely that vehicles built before 2012 have ABS. To check the earlier vehicles that might not have ABS, examine the dashboard lights as the vehicle is started. If there is a light that says ABS, that vehicle has the system. If the light goes out after starting, the system is working properly. It's important for the student to know the type of braking system on any vehicle the student drives because it changes the appropriate driver actions in an emergency stop.

The electronics in a vehicle with ABS will prevent the vehicle brakes from locking (stop turning) while the vehicle is still in motion above 1 or 2 mph. That means the brakes will not start a slide no matter how hard the brakes are pushed. The system does not, however, add traction between the tire and the pavement; it only maximizes the braking system. It will keep the vehicle stopping in the direction the vehicle is heading, whether straight or turning. Since there is a physical limit to the amount of friction between the tire and the pavement, if some friction is being used for turning, there will be less available for braking. That means that if it is braking that's needed, it's done best in a straight line.

Set two markers about 40 feet apart (approximately 14-15 paces) along the line where the student can drive 25 mph.

Demonstrate an emergency stop from 25 mph or 30 mph, braking at the first cone.

Make sure the stop is hard enough to engage the ABS. The student will be hanging off the seat belt with a big grin from enjoying the G force of the stop. If this is the first emergency stop the student has experienced, s/he will be impressed with how much force it generates and you will never have an issue with seat belt usage by the student.

Point out to the student where the vehicle has stopped in relation to the second marker and tell her/him the distance between the markers.

Explanation

It is important to tell a student that braking is not the same for all speeds, conditions and vehicles. Typical sedans can stop from 30 mph in about 35 feet on dry pavement. That distance is braking only, neglecting the reaction time it requires to see the problem and move the foot. Sedans doing emergency braking from 60 mph to 30 mph take, on average, about 3 feet to slow 1 mph. So the total stopping distance from 60 mph will be in the range of 125-130 feet. Sedans doing emergency braking from 80 mph to 60 mph take, on average, more than 5 feet to slow 1 mph in that speed range. So it takes more than 100 feet longer to stop from 80 mph than from 60 mph, braking as hard as the ABS system can take.

An emergency stop on wet pavement is about double the distance. SUV's take longer to stop than sedans, pickups longer still, and vehicles built for off-road travel with drum brakes take the longest.

Switch seats with the student and have the student make 3 successful emergency stops from 25 mph or 30 mph.

> Some students are very timid about using the vehicle hard and may need encouragement to perform. It's good to know that before driving on the roads, but for everyone's sake, the student needs to make successful emergency stops. For some students, using the term "stand on it" gets the point across. If the student can't bring him/herself to brake hard after three attempts, tell the student you are going to help him/her. Tell the student your help will be to yell at them and that will make him/her stop fast. On the next run <u>do just that</u>, loudly yell, "BRAKE" and that should make the stop happen.

State road test requirements will include several driving maneuvers not used often, like the three-point turn, or K-turn. This would be an appropriate time to practice them briefly to ease the student's mind about being able to accomplish them.

When the student has reasonable control of the gas and brake pedals, appears to steer okay, especially on right turns, and is not too timid about speed and braking, it's time to drive on a neighborhood road. If the control is not present, continue practice in the parking lot.

If the first place the student is going to drive on the road is not adjacent to the parking lot, the teacher should drive the vehicle to the practice area.

Put the student behind the wheel. Then have the student adjust the mirrors if necessary.

Next, direct the student to put the vehicle in gear, check for traffic, and start driving.

Note

Some suburban subdivisions don't have stop signs at every intersection, so call an imaginary stop sign when needed.

Tell the student where to look.

Explanation

You will need to explain to the student that s/he should look primarily far ahead of the vehicle to become aware of situations before they happen. The student's eyes should be busy, looking for the most part far down the road but also looking closer to the vehicle to see potholes, debris, animals beside the road, curves, and pedestrians as the long-distance looks warn them of those potential hazards. You will not need to watch the student's eyes to see if s/he is looking ahead or right in front of the vehicle.

If the student's hands are very busy making left-right-left-right adjustments to the steering wheel to stay in the lane, it means that the student is looking right in front of the vehicle. When the focus is farther ahead, the student makes fewer and smaller adjustments to keep within the lane.

When the student is approaching parked cars, tell him/her to look under them for feet or animals. Doing so may give an early warning of something about to enter your path.

At the first occasion for a right turn, make sure there is no car approaching. If there is a car that could be in the way, have the student stop (unless you are using a passenger side brake) before the turn. Otherwise, tell the student "Signal, slow, turn, straighten, resume." Repeat this mantra for the first few turns.

Make the first road session short if there was a parking lot session as well. Driving lessons are stressful for new drivers.

Note

When the student makes an error, explain to the student right then why s/he wasn't successful. When the same situation comes again, remind the student of the solution in advance so the student can be successful. Compliment on what was done well and on improvements. The teacher must make an effort to notice when the student corrects a problem. The solutions to the mistakes the student make should also be practiced ahead of time at the start of the next lesson.

Typical turning mistakes and their solutions

Symptom: Slowing too much in turns

Cause: Nervousness, lack of experience, and lack of confidence
Solution: Practice is the answer to all the causes. The experienced driver turns at about 12 mph. Concentrate on a steady speed during the turn. The student's turning speed will increase naturally.

<u>Symptom</u>: **Hitting the curb with the rear wheel on right turns**

<u>Cause</u>: (1) Turns too soon

<u>Solution</u>: Start to turn when the curb or corner disappears from view in the right corner of the windshield

<u>Cause</u>: (2) Starts the turn with the vehicle too close to the curb

<u>Solution</u>: The turn can be done better by starting from the center of the lane

<u>Symptom</u>: **Crossing the center line of the new road in right turn, making a big turn to the right and a big turn to the left**

<u>Cause</u>: (1) Starts the turn too close to the curb.

<u>Solution</u>: The turn can be done better by starting from the center of the lane.

<u>Cause</u>: (2) Delays the quarter-turn-motion part of the turn.

<u>Solution</u>: Explain to the student that the turning motion is a one-two action. First comes the half turn with both hands on the wheel and then the right hand grabs the wheel at the 12 o'clock position and pulls the wheel down. There is no pause in the one-two.

<u>Cause</u>: (3) It might also occur because the student is looking at the center line instead of the lane.

<u>Solution</u>: Remind the student that the car will go where the driver is looking so the driver should look at the lane of the new road.

Cause: (4) Pulling the vehicle close to the crossing street to see any oncoming traffic made the turn very tight.

Solution: For a very tight right turn, tell the student to start turning the wheel <u>before</u> applying the gas.

Cause: (5) Turns too late.

Solution: Start to turn when the curb or corner disappears from view in the right corner of the windshield.

Symptom: Taking too long to get speed back up after a turn

Cause: Thinking about the just completed turn

Solution: Remind the student to increase speed back to the travel speed as soon as the turn is completed. Explain that the others using the road and catching up behind are already traveling at that speed.

Symptom: Straightening the steering wheel too soon coming out of a turn.

Cause: Lack of experience and a worry that a lot of hand speed is needed to turn the steering wheel in time.

Solution: Assure the student that waiting until the vehicle is headed straight in the driving lane will leave enough time to straighten the steering wheel.

(B) <u>Teaching a student who has had some experience</u>

When a teacher starts training a student who has had some experience, it's wise to assess the student's skills before going on the road.

There may be some bad habits to correct or perhaps the student isn't catching on to an important action.

The skills to be assessed are brake and gas application, steering, and use of the eyes. The place to conduct the assessment should be a large parking lot. Before arriving at the training area, ask the student the driving experience s/he has: types of road driven on (local, four-lane, interstate, etc.); highest speed driven; how many hours driven; any crashes; how recent is the experience. Sometimes what looks like a lack of skill is merely "rust" that won't last long. Ask the student if there is anything special s/he wants to work on. That will tell you a lot about the training needs.

At the parking lot, explain that you will use several exercises to start the lessons.

First Exercise: Slalom

Equipment needs – Five traffic cones or milk jugs or small cardboard boxes. Putting some sand or water in the jugs/boxes will keep them anchored. Don't fill completely or seal the containers during the exercise. They should be allowed to collapse easily.

Exercise layout

Place the five objects in a straight line about 40 feet apart (about 14 paces) from each other for small sedans, farther apart for pickups and long wheelbase vehicles. Leave room in the parking lot to turn at each end. To make the line straight, use the principle of going where you're looking. That is, look at some object in the distance and walk directly toward it, dropping the markers at the right distances as you go.

Exercise operation

Drive the length of the obstacle line at a modest speed, weaving between each of the objects in a slalom fashion. Come as close to the obstacles with the rear wheel as possible. While passing the last obstacle, make a turn away from the line far enough to allow for the turning circle of the vehicle. Then turn the opposite way, basically making a wide circle, to end the turn in position to weave through the slalom in the opposite direction back to the starting point. Make a wide circle at the end to line the vehicle up for the student to follow the same path.

Driving position

Have the student get into the driver's seat while you are outside the car with the driver's door open. Show the student the seat adjustment controls and guide the student into proper positioning. The ideal seating position will have the student's eyes about half-way up the windshield. The student's breastbone should be at least 10 inches back from the airbag in the steering wheel. The student should be close enough to the pedals to be able to comfortably press the brake as hard as possible with the right foot without shifting in the seat. Then adjust the steering wheel so the student's elbow bend is 90 to 120 degrees and at a comfortable height when holding the steering wheel at the 10 and 2 positions as on a clock face. The back of the head should not be touching the head restraint. The seat belt must go over the shoulder to be effective.

Explanation

If the student isn't tall enough, a seat cushion is called for.

The airbag deploys at 200 mph for 10 inches to protect the head and face in a crash and then deflates. It's difficult to estimate what 10 inches looks like so use this solution: spread your fingers as far apart as possible and measure the distance between the outside of the thumb to the outside of the pinky. You'll likely find it to be 7 or 8 inches. Compare your finger spread to the student's and then the student will have a portable measurement standard.

Right foot braking is recommended. In an emergency, the driver who uses left foot braking is likely to press the brake with the left foot and the gas with the right foot with unfortunate results. The heel of the right foot should remain on the floor for ordinary driving levels. The foot can then flex left and right between the brake pedal and the gas pedal and control of both pedals is managed with the calf muscles of the leg, not the quadriceps. This means that high heeled shoes should not be worn on the right foot when driving. Whatever style of shoe is worn on the right foot, it should have a strap or heel surround of some type. That strap/surround will keep the shoe on the foot when moving rapidly between gas and brake in an emergency.

Auto companies design the steering wheels with spokes at what would be the 9 and 3 positions on a clock face and thickened areas above the 10 and 2 positions, thus giving the 10 and 2 positions space to grip the wheel more securely when grip is needed and a place to rest the thumbs. The hands should always remain on the outside of the steering wheel. The 9 and 3 position on the steering wheel is ok but not as good as the 10 and 2.

Both positions allow a quick half-turn of the wheel with one motion. If the arms are too straight in front of the student (beyond 120 degrees), the student will develop pain in the upper shoulder area when doing long driving stints.

The head should not be touching the head restraint because when the head is resting on the head restraint, head-turning motions are restricted and the vibrations in the car jiggle the eyes. Some hairstyles just don't work for driving normal vehicles. Ponytails positioned on the back of the head contact the head restraint and are a constant annoyance, and tall hair styles can rub on the roof of the vehicle, making the student a bit claustrophobic. Hair styles that frame the face often block peripheral vision so there needs to be a way to keep the hair back while driving. Tucking the hair behind the ears doesn't work long enough.

A few students may try to wear just the lap portion of the seat belt which, of course, is not adequate. The teacher must insist on wearing the seat belt properly in the beginning. An exercise provided later will be the convincing argument.

Left and right

You may be surprised to find that students confuse left and right. It happens more often with people for whom English is not their native language. Luckily there is a reminder in the car. The outside mirror adjustment mechanisms on the door or on the dashboard are labeled

"L" and "R" in the correct relative positions and are a good reminder to the students every time they enter the car.

Starting the vehicle

From inside the vehicle, show the student how to start it.

Note

If the vehicle starts with a key, it's possible that the steering wheel lock will engage and not allow the key to turn. This is a good time to explain the steering wheel lock's purpose (anti-theft and prevent accidentally rolling into traffic when parked) and how to wiggle the wheel while turning the key to get the engine started. It's also a good time to explain that a key ring loaded with keys and souvenirs can accidently be brushed by the knee in a way that turns the engine off and locks the steering wheel while the car is still moving.

Show the student that the tachometer (on the dashboard) measures the speed of the engine's turning.

Note

When a warmed-up gasoline engine is running at idle, the tachometer will show the engine turning about 750 revolutions per minute (RPM's). A cold engine will idle faster.

Tell the student to put the vehicle into gear and proceed to weave through the slalom at a modest pace, trying to come close to the obstacles with the rear wheel and placing the rear wheel the same distance to the obstacles whether turning left or right.

Note

The teacher should watch for other traffic in the parking lot and at the same time be aware of how the student is turning the steering wheel and controlling the vehicle.

Explanation of the slalom exercise

The student will show his/her vehicle handling skill in this exercise. It involves looking where the vehicle should go, steering motions, and gas/brake control, as well as matching hand speed to vehicle speed in the tight turns.

The desirable steering method is the hand-over-hand, the front of the vehicle should cross the line of obstacles in about the middle of each two obstacles and the speed should be steady. If the student is not producing those results, don't let him/her continue driving incorrectly and practicing the wrong things.

Typical mistakes and their solutions

<u>Symptom:</u> **Steering too far in each direction and thus not traveling close to the obstacles.**

<u>Cause:</u> It could be "rust" but more likely it's due to inexperience with that level of vehicle handling.

<u>Solution:</u> Have the student stop the vehicle, then drive forward slowly with the teacher telling the student when to turn and when to stop turning. That will give the

student a reminder of correct steering and reference points of when to turn.

Symptom: Failing to get around all the obstacles.

Cause: The student did not start the turns with two hands and then go to hand-over-hand steering.

Solution: Hand-over-hand steering results in a half turn of the steering wheel with one motion, which makes it fast without having to hurry the hands. When it's followed closely by a quarter turn, the student will be able to move the hands fast enough to make good turns in sync with the normal speeds. Practice the turning motions while the vehicle is stopped, then incorporate the motion in traveling through the slalom. The student may have difficulty "unlearning" some previous style of steering.

Symptom: Hitting the obstacles on one side of the vehicle.

Cause: The student doesn't realize the size of the vehicle or have a reference point to calculate the distance to an obstacle.

Solution: Place the vehicle parallel to the line of obstacles just far enough away to clear the obstacles and have the student drive straight along the obstacles (not hitting) so the student can select a reference point on the vehicle (wiper blade, dashboard mark, vehicle bodywork, etc.) which will indicate to him/her where the wheels are in relation to the obstacles.

Symptom: Pushing the gas hard, then the brake, then the gas, and so on.

> **Cause:** Probably not keeping the heel on the floor and using the calf muscles to control the pedals.
>
> **Solution:** Call the student's attention to keeping the heel on the floor. It may require moving the seat forward and the steering wheel higher.

If proper steering is going to require the student to change steering methods, don't expect instant success. Try to get one or two successful turns then move on. This is assessment, so tell the student that steering will need to be worked on, then change seats with the student for the next demonstration.

Drive through the obstacle course as fast as possible, but just in one direction, using the hand-over-hand steering to demonstrate that hand-over-hand steering is the fastest form of steering. That demonstration will help the student adopt the style of steering which can avoid crashes better than other steering styles.

Second Exercise

The teacher is now at the end of the slalom line opposite the start. Proceed toward the exercise start but stop at the second obstacle (cone) you come to and change it (tip it over, move it noticeably out of line, etc.) then drive to the start. When viewing the line of obstacles from the start of the slalom line, the tipped cone will be the fourth one in the line. This exercise is for emergency braking.

This is an appropriate time to practice emergency braking. The student will make many mistakes, and that is an expectation of the student as well. Practicing what to do in an emergency will give the student confidence that s/he can do the right thing in an emergency and that mistakes are accepted.

Explanation of the emergency braking exercise

Explain Antilock Braking System (ABS) to the student.

Note

The owner's manual should have a description or use this one. All vehicles built in 2012 and later must have ABS and it is likely that vehicles built before 2012 have ABS. To check the earlier vehicles that might not have ABS, examine the dashboard lights when the vehicle is started. If a light appears that says ABS, that vehicle has the system. If the light goes out after starting, the system is working properly.

The electronics in the vehicle will prevent the vehicle brakes from locking (stop turning) while the vehicle is still in motion above 1 or 2 mph. That means the brakes will not start a slide no matter how hard the brakes are pushed. The system does not, however, add traction between the tire and the pavement; it maximizes the braking system. It will keep the vehicle stopping in the direction the vehicle is heading, whether straight or turning. Since there is a physical limit to the amount of friction between the tire and the pavement, if some friction is being used for turning, there will be less available for braking. That means that if it is braking that's needed, it's done best in a straight line.

Demonstrate an emergency stop from 25 mph or 30 mph, braking at the fourth obstacle which was the changed one.

Note

> Make sure that the stop is hard enough to engage the ABS. The student will be hanging off the seat belt with a big grin from enjoying the G force of the stop. If this is the first emergency stop the student has experienced, s/he will be impressed with how much force it generates and you will never have an issue with seat belt usage by the student.

Point out to the student where the vehicle has stopped in relation to the fifth obstacle and tell her/him the distance between the markers.

Note

> It is important to tell a student that braking is not the same for all speeds, conditions and vehicles. Typical sedans can stop from 30 mph in about 35 feet on dry pavement. That distance is braking only, neglecting the reaction time it requires to see the problem and move the foot. Sedans doing emergency braking from 60 mph to 30 mph take, on average, about 3 feet to slow 1 mph. So the total stopping distance from 60 mph will be in the range of 125-130 feet. Sedans doing emergency braking from 80 mph to 60 mph take, on average, more than 5 feet to slow 1 mph in that speed range. So it takes more than 100 feet longer to stop from 80 mph than from 60 mph, braking as hard as the ABS system can take.

An emergency stop on wet pavement is about double the distance. SUV's take longer to stop than sedans, pickups longer still, and vehicles built for off-road travel with drum brakes take the longest.

Switch seats with the student and have the student attempt emergency stops from 25 mph or 30 mph. Run the exercise in one direction only. To keep the brakes from overheating and warping the rotors of disc brakes, have the student return to the start without holding the brake pedal down for a long period. If discussion of the stop is needed, have the student put the vehicle in "Park." Three successful emergency stops will be enough.

Note

Some students are very timid about using the vehicle hard and may need encouragement to perform. It's good to know that before driving on the roads. For some students, using the term "stand on it" gets the point across. If the student can't bring him/herself to brake hard after three attempts, tell the student you are going to help him/her. Tell the student your help will be to yell at them and that will make him/her stop fast. Then do just that, loudly, yell "BRAKE" and that should make the stop happen.

After emergency stops, collect the obstacles used in the two exercises.

Backing exercise

Find an area where there will be plenty of space behind the vehicle then tell the student to stop and put the car into "park". Explain that

(1) when going forward, the driver steers in the direction s/he wants the front of the vehicle to go; (2) when backing the driver steers in the direction s/he wants the back to go. Most beginners think it must be harder than that. Check to see that there is plenty of space and tell the driver to put the vehicle into "reverse." Let the student keep the backing speed slow and try steering left and right to confirm that steering in the direction s/he wants the back to go is correct. There are only two possible directions so if one way is wrong, the other must be right. For some students, it works to have them look where they want the back of the vehicle to go and then steer in the direction they are looking.

This is the time to explain to the student that drivers tend to steer in the direction they are looking.

Explanation

> The driver needs to look where the driver <u>does</u> want the vehicle to go – not where s/he <u>doesn't</u> want to go. Humans use their eyes for aiming. That's something we know from sports and games. So if drivers look at what they don't want to hit (debris, pothole, curb, etc.), they are likely to hit what they are looking at. Other common examples: A driver looking to the right to see his/her phone will steer toward the right, recover and do it again. Drivers steer toward pedestrians and lighted police cars they are looking at intently.

State road test requirements will include several driving maneuvers not used often, like the three-point turn, or K-turn. This would be an appropriate time to practice these maneuvers briefly to ease the student's mind about being able to accomplish them.

Assessment result

If the student has reasonable control of the gas and brake pedals, steers well most of the time, especially on right turns, and is not too timid about speed and braking, it's time to move to the next stage and drive on a neighborhood road. There will probably not be enough time remaining in the scheduled lesson to continue to a neighborhood. Explain that the lesson is over and that you and the student will either start the next lesson in a neighborhood, or if you conclude that the student is not yet capable of driving on a neighborhood road with your guidance, explain that the lesson is over and that you and the student will return to the practice lot for the start of the next lesson.

Chapter Two

···✦·✦·✦·✦···

Neighborhood Driving

Planning

You'll want to find a neighborhood with a variety of intersection types, low traffic at the time of the lesson, good roadway signage, some hills and valleys, and differently shaped curves. Naturally, the perfect neighborhood doesn't exist.

If you are teaching individuals, you should plan on a one-hour lesson. The student experiences a high level of stress at this stage and that affects the driving performance. Driving much longer than one hour causes the student to lose concentration, and the net result is the student practices a lot of mistakes in the second hour.

If there is mist or light rain, the lesson should still be held. Visibility at neighborhood speeds, both forward and backward, will not be appreciably affected and it offers an opportunity to discuss hydroplaning.

Explanation of hydroplaning

Hydroplaning occurs when water is pushed in front of a tire like a wave and the tire (and the vehicle attached to it) rides up on the wave, causing the tire to lose contact with the ground. Passenger vehicles in general can hydroplane beginning in the 45-50 mph range if the tire has no tread and there is standing water on the road. Standing water can be identified by its shiny surface like a puddle. So the primary variables involved are speed, tire tread and the depth of water on the road. Other factors are weight on the tire, whether the vehicle is turning, and whether two tires on the same end of the vehicle lose contact with the road at the same time.

Here are two scenarios:

A passenger vehicle traveling on a straight part of the interstate, riding on tires with more than the minimum tread will not hydroplane unless the standing water level becomes deep, like driving through a deep puddle. Even if the vehicle hydroplanes both front wheels, momentum will keep the vehicle going straight until the vehicle lands back on earth.

An unloaded pickup truck on tires with good tread driving on a curving interstate in the rain might hydroplane in standing water or a puddle. On a curve, the lightly weighted rear wheels will not be following in the tracks made by the front wheels and that means the rear wheels will ride up on the wave more easily.

With both rear wheels not touching the earth on a curve, the rear of the vehicle will start to spin to the outside of the curve. The same scene will develop for passenger vehicles that are based on a pickup chassis.

Make sure the student is properly seated, then practice the steering motions, i.e. making left and right half circle turns with both hands on the wheel.

Make sure the student knows how to use the signals.

Driving

Then direct the student to put the vehicle in gear, check for traffic, and start driving.

Note

Some subdivisions don't have stop signs at every inter-section, so call an imaginary stop sign when needed.

Tell the student where to look.

Explanation of where to look

You will need to explain to the student that s/he should look primarily far ahead of the vehicle to become aware of situations before they happen. The student's eyes should be busy, looking for the most part far down the road, but also looking closer to the vehicle to see potholes, debris, animals beside the road, curves, and pedestrians. The long-distance looks warn them of those potential hazards, and they will need to steer around them. You will not need to watch the student's eyes to see if s/he is looking ahead or right in front of the vehicle. If the student's hands are very busy making left-right-left-right adjustments to the steering wheel to stay in the lane, it means that the student is looking right in front of the vehicle. When the main focus is farther ahead, the student makes fewer and smaller adjustments.

When driving in a cul-de-sac or on a roundabout, the driver should be looking to the left ahead of the vehicle.

When the student is approaching parked cars, tell him/her to look under them for feet or animals. Doing so may give an early warning of something about to enter your path.

Tell the student that the ordinary position for the vehicle is in the center of the lane.

Discuss the other occasions.

Explanation of lane placement

Driving in the center of the lane leaves space on either side of the vehicle in case the driver wanders a bit or something suddenly appears at the side of the road. It leaves sufficient room to safely pass other vehicles in the opposing lanes. If there are pedestrians to avoid, the student should move to the left about half a lane width, thus both giving the pedestrian room and also not going too far into the opposing lane. If there is a parked vehicle or similar obstacle and there is opposing traffic, the vehicle whose side the obstacle is on should be the one to slow or stop as necessary. The basic rule of thumb is, if the problem is on the student's side of the road, the student should make the adjustment.

Lane management problems at slow speed

Symptom: Wandering from one side of the lane to the other even though looking ahead.

Cause: (1) Steering inputs too large.

Solution: Practice part of one lesson in a cemetery or a similar location where the roads are one-way and narrow to accustom the student to less movement.

Cause: (2) One hand higher on the steering wheel than the other.

Solution: Instruct the student to keep his/her hands at the same height on the steering wheel when driving straight.

At the first right turn tell the student "to signal (right), slow, turn 1,2, straighten, and resume speed".

Check the signal indicator on the dashboard to make sure the signal is for the correct direction.

Explanation of turning instructions

The student studied the driving rules for a license exam at some point, but it was an academic environment. Being behind-the-wheel now requires application of that knowledge, and many students have trouble using academic knowledge in street situations.

For example, for the first right turn your student makes, you will need to tell him/her when to signal.

S/he can answer a test question about signaling but still not know when to do it in the real world, or that the signal should come before braking. There will be a state rule about how far ahead of an intersection a driver should signal, but you will not find a student who has measured to find what that distance looks like through a vehicle windshield.

"Turn 1,2" refers, on a right turn, to the half turn of the steering wheel with both hands (the "1") and the immediate follow-up of the half turn (the "2") made by moving the right hand to the 12 o'clock position on the steering wheel and pulling it down.

Most beginners will anticipate the need for straightening the steering wheel and steer left too soon. Advise the student to wait until the vehicle is aligned with the new path of travel before straightening. That advice will ensure the student is looking ahead in the new lane of travel

Beginning drivers thinking about what to do with their hands will often neglect using their feet to maintain speed during the turn. The abrupt slowing often done by beginners could cause a following driver to hit the student's vehicle. The student needs to be reminded to keep a steady speed during the turn. It won't happen immediately.

The student may need reminding to turn the signal switch off.

Turning mistakes

Symptom: Slowing too much in turns.

> **Cause:** Nervousness, lack of experience, and lack of confidence.
>
> **Solution:** Practice is the answer to all the causes. The experienced driver turns at about 12 mph. Concentrate on a steady speed during the turn. The speed will increase naturally.

Symptom: Hitting the curb with the rear wheel on right turns.

> **Cause:** (1) Turns too soon.
>
> **Solution**: Start to turn when the curb or corner disappears from view in the right corner of the windshield.
>
> **Cause:** (2) Starts the turn with the vehicle too close to the curb.
>
> **Solution:** The turn can be done better by starting from the center of the lane, or in extremely tight turns, from the left side of the lane.

Symptom: Crossing the center line of the new road in a right turn, making a big turn to the right and a big turn to the left.

> **Cause:** (1) Starts the turn too close to the curb.
>
> **Solution:** The turn can be done better by starting from the center of the lane.

Cause: (2) Delays the quarter-turn-motion part of the turn.

Solution: Explain to the student that the turning motion is a one-two action. First comes the half turn with both hands on the wheel and then the right grabs the wheel at the 12 o'clock position and pulls the wheel down. There is no pause in the one-two.

Cause: (3) It might also occur because the student is looking at the center line instead of the lane.

Solution: Remind the student that the car will go where the driver is looking so the driver should look at the lane of the new road.

Cause: (4) Pulling the vehicle close to the crossing street to see any oncoming traffic made the turn very tight.

Solution: For a very tight right turn, tell the student to steer the wheel <u>before</u> applying the gas.

Symptom: Straightening the steering wheel too soon coming out of a turn.

Cause: Lack of experience and a worry that a lot of hand speed is needed to turn the wheel in time.

Solution: Assure the student that waiting until the vehicle is headed straight in the lane before straightening the steering wheel will still leave plenty of time to complete the action.

Symptom: Taking too long to get speed back up after a turn.

Cause: Thinking about the just completed turn.

Solution: Remind the student to increase speed back to the travel speed as soon as the turn is completed. Explain that the others using the road and catching up are already traveling at that speed.

When approaching the first left turn remind the student that left turns are not as sharp as a right turn so the amount of steering input will be less and the speed of turning slightly slower.

You will still need to say "Signal, slow, turn, straighten, resume speed."

The student must not intrude on the left lane space of the new road. If the left lane is marked by painted lines, tell the student "Go around the paint."

Note

> Driving lessons are stressful for new drivers. When the student makes an error, explain to the student right then why the error happened. Then remind the student of the solution <u>in advance</u> the next time the situation occurs so the student can be successful. Compliment on what was done well and on improvements. The teacher must make an effort to notice when the student corrects a problem. The solutions to the mistakes the student makes can be practiced ahead of time at the start of the next lesson.

Let the student try stopping on his/her own if it's safe to do so. After the student has tried a few stops, review with the student the state rules for stopping because the student has probably forgotten them.

Then inform the student how to stop gently.

Explanation of gentle stopping

The heel of the right foot should remain on the floor for ordinary driving levels. The foot can then flex left and right between the brake pedal and the gas pedal and control of both pedals is managed with the calf muscles of the leg, not the thigh muscles.

To make a smooth, gentle stop, the student should slow and then just before the vehicle stops, ease the pressure on the brake pedal. That slight easing will result in stopping from 2 or 3 mph instead of from 10 mph, making the stop much gentler.

If there is a hill steep enough to use, show the student how to start from an intersection on a hill without rolling backwards.

Explanation of starting on a hill

Let's assume that the vehicle is on a hill at a stop. If the vehicle is not equipped with a working "hill holder" option, there are two possible ways for the driver to keep the vehicle from rolling backward when trying to start on a hill.

The first method to prevent rollback consists of moving the left foot to the left edge of the brake pedal and applying enough pressure to keep the vehicle in place. Then move the right foot to the gas pedal. When it is time to move forward, the driver applies light pressure to the gas pedal while easing pressure on the brake pedal until it is released. The vehicle moves forward as planned without rolling backward.

The second method of starting on a hill consists of applying the hand operated parking (emergency) brake tightly after the stop. When it is time to move forward, release the parking brake gradually while pushing the gas pedal.

If the vehicle has a clutch, using the parking brake method is easiest. Another way, in a manual shift vehicle, is to use the <u>side of the right foot</u>, the foot on the brake, to press the gas pedal as the left lets the clutch out.

Explain to the student that driving at a steady speed is economical, on one hand, and good manners on the other hand, if there are other vehicles behind. Explain that steady speed is different from keeping gas pedal in the same position. In other words, to maintain a steady speed, the driver must ease the pressure on the gas when going downhill and press the gas pedal harder when going uphill.

The remainder of the neighborhood practice should emphasize driving through the neighborhood gradually working up toward traveling at the neighborhood speed limit (typically 25 mph), making better and better turns and complete stops in the right location.

Find a place to safely practice the three-point (or "K") turn, or other turn-about in the street as presented in the state rules.

The safe place will have enough room to complete the action and it will be in a spot that is visible by other drivers in time for them to stop if needed.

Find a safe place to practice backing while staying in the lane.

Find a street with good visibility by other drivers and with clear markings of the center line and edge of the lane.

To back the vehicle and stay in the lane, the student should use both outside rear-view mirrors. Looking in only one mirror or looking at a rear-view camera screen may cause an inexperienced driver to keep the head turned toward the information source. The student will then tend to turn the steering wheel in the direction he/she is looking and drive out of the lane.

Tell the student to stay between the center and edge of the lane while backing.

Discuss what to do if a pet, farm animal or wild animal runs into the road.

Animal in the road

There will be more than one opinion on what to do about an animal in the road, but whatever that opinion is, discuss it and plan what to do before it happens. There won't be time to think things through while it is happening.

Here's one view; It's fine to avoid or stop for squirrels, rabbits and other small animals, if possible, but not at the cost of harming a human. That means you don't slam on the brakes when there is a vehicle behind you or turn toward another vehicle or run off the road just to save a bunny. A cow or a deer, however, can wreck the vehicle, so stopping or avoiding large animals is the best idea. Nearby drivers are likely to see the large animals too.

When to move on from neighborhoods to two-lane roads

Staying too long in neighborhood driving affects the student's judgment of how much and how fast the steering wheel is moved to keep in the proper lane. Slower speeds in the neighborhood use relatively big motions, but at higher speeds, the wheel should move less. If the student becomes too used to the slow speed, adjusting to higher speeds takes more time.

The student needs to have the basic vehicle handling skills become almost automatic before the teacher can expect the student to be aware of what other traffic is doing and develop the skill of looking in the mirrors.

When the student is signaling, slowing, turning, straightening, and resuming speed nearly all the time without reminders and making the turns safely, even if not perfectly every time, consider moving up to driving on local two-lane roads. Of course, the student should be comfortable driving at the neighborhood speed limit. Basically, the student needs to be predictable enough to be trusted behind the wheel.

Chapter Three

···✦✦✦···

Two-Lane Roads

The ideal two-lane road or combination of roads, for training new drivers will be wide enough to have painted lane markings, a speed limit of about 30 mph to 40 mph, light traffic at the time of the lesson, maintain the same character for 10 or 15 miles, and have uncomplicated intersections. The teacher should know the road well enough in advance to be able to prepare the student for the new situations as they are approached.

The teacher needs to refresh his/her memory of the sign meanings, what to do at 4-way stops or on roundabouts, of any "move over" laws, or what action to take if an emergency vehicle is approaching.

Attention problems

When the student was a passenger, s/he was able to look at scenery, interesting architecture, attractive persons on the sidewalks, etc., with full attention. Now, as a driver, such long glances are dangerous. Driving must now come first in priority. Whenever looking away from the road, the student needs to take quick looks, then return attention to the road.

The driver tends to drive in the direction the driver is looking so the teacher will know what the student is looking at by where the steering takes the vehicle.

Entering the roadway

Let the student have the first chance at choosing when to enter the road. If the student takes too long or waits for too large a gap in traffic, then advise when it is safe.

Advise the student to accelerate to the speed limit right away.

Tell the student to drive in the middle of the lane. Staying within the lane requires attention and skill. The experienced driver maintains position in the lane without a thought on how to do it, but the student has to work at it.

Lane Keeping Problems

Symptom: Moving the wheel too much, sawing back and forth.

> **Cause: (1)** If the movement is constant, the student is looking right in front of the vehicle. **Solution:** Tell the student to look farther ahead.

> **Cause: (2)** If the movement is two moves, one in each direction with a pause in between, then two moves again, the student is steering too much on the first input and then correcting it.

Solution: Tell the student that as the vehicle speed increases, the steering inputs need to be smaller.

Symptom; Steering from one side of the lane to the other like zigzagging or tacking.

Cause: Alternating between looking at the left then right edges of the lane instead of the center of the lane.
Solution: Tell the student to look farther ahead at the center of the lane.

Symptom: Hugging one side of the lane or the other.

Cause: The student may fear oncoming traffic or running off the road.
Solution: If the student stays on the right side of the lane, let the student know how much room there is to the left by telling the student to steer the left side wheels over the yellow "Bott's dots" (small reflectors) in the yellow paint separating the opposing traffic flows. The student will be very surprised at how much room is available. If the student stays to the left side of the lane, tell the student to drive over something to the right. There may be "dots" or rumble strips, or you could direct the student to deliberately run off the edge of the road (in a safe place, of course). Tell the student to choose reference points on the vehicle like the end of a wiper blade, a windshield washer nozzle, or other features to use as reference points to estimate where the wheels are going to travel.

Telling the student to drive the speed limit helps focus attention to the speed limit signs.   Call the student's attention to the other signs as well because the student has spent years ignoring them.

Discuss safe following distances with the student.

Explanation

The recommended safe following distance is typically expressed in seconds behind the vehicle in front of you. It is measured by watching the vehicle in front pass some marker, like a dashed lane marker or feature of the road, and counting the time until your vehicle passes the same marker. By using time as the measure, the distance automatically adjusts with the speed. The safe following distance remained at 2 seconds for a long time. It was based on the premise that realizing an emergency stopping situation was required and then physically reacting to it took about 1 second. That left about 1 second to spare in case attention was elsewhere at the start. Recently, the recommended safe following distance was increased to 3 seconds in some standard texts without explanation. Yet in real life, traffic has increased and vehicle braking has improved to the point that a 1 second distance between vehicles is commonly seen, and a 3 second space between vehicles in traffic seems to invite lane jumping.

A single measure for all vehicles is not a true guide because different types of vehicles have different stopping abilities. Sports cars stop much faster than tractor trailers as an example. That means that the best answer to "What is a safe following distance?" is, "It depends."

You could start with the 2 second rule of thumb and then modify it to fit the situation. For instance if you're following a vehicle that can stop like yours does, the 2 seconds should be safe enough. If, however, you can see from the shadows of the two cars ahead of you that the vehicle in front of you is tailgating the car ahead of it, leave more time. In another case, if the vehicle behind you is tailgating, you should leave more time ahead of you. That would be done so you can apply brakes gently at first to give longer warning to the vehicle behind you before you brake hard. If you look through the windows of the vehicle ahead of you, you can see the upper brake light of the vehicle two ahead of you. It can give you an earlier warning. If you are following a vehicle with the brake lights always on, leave more time because the warning effect of the brake lights going on is now gone. And so on.

The student may choose to look at the speedometer or in the mirrors at inappropriate times, i.e. in a turn or on a curve. The teacher should take care not to call the student's attention to the speed if it isn't safe to check it. It is safer to check the speed when the road is straight and there is no traffic.

Maintaining a steady speed is helped by attending to the sounds of the wind noise, engine noise, and tire noise. Changes in sound or vibration mean the speed has changed. With more experience the new driver will be able to notice when the speed changes without looking at the speedometer.

The student will worry about taking curves at the higher speeds. Explain that the speed limit signs have the road variations factored in. The sight line, road surface, and corner radius have already been considered. If there is an unusual situation, there will be a warning sign.

The student may apply the brake in the middle of a curve. However, braking before the curve is much safer. Traction is used for both braking and turning so it's best to do them separately. It is especially important to separate braking and turning when the road is slick.

This is a good time for the student to add the skill of looking in the rear-view mirrors to check on the driving situation behind the vehicle. As with checking the speedometer, the student needs to take only a quick look before returning the eyes to the driving task.

It would be beneficial for the student to encounter a construction zone while driving at these lower speeds and learn the customs involved.

Remind the student of the general rules of the state in regard to making way for emergency vehicles.

Remind the student of the actions to take, and actions to not take, when told to pull over by police.

The student has probably never planned which roads to take to get to a particular destination. Now the student will need to start learning street names, directions and estimating driving time. Explain how to determine where s/he is when lost and what to do about it.

If the road meets the other criteria, conduct the lesson on a route the student will likely take after getting the license. Make it sort of a rehearsal.

Try to locate an intersection where the student will need to cross a multi-lane road without the benefit of a traffic light.

Explanation

> Generally a multi-lane road without a traffic light will have a turn lane or a turn lane and median separating the opposing lanes. A student without experience might try to wait until all the lanes are clear in both directions. What should happen is the student should wait for the nearest set of lanes to clear (traffic from the left), accelerate to the middle area between the sets of lanes and stop, or slow enough to see that the traffic from the right lanes leaves enough space to continue crossing with safety. Then proceed with crossing the final set of lanes.

To move on to the next step, the student should be able to keep the vehicle within the lane, notice and follow roads signs, safely make a turn to a new road from about 40 mph, not flinch at opposing traffic, be able to mostly maintain a steady speed, and generally seem at ease with the higher speeds.

Before the next lesson on multi-lane roads, the student should review the section of the state driving manual concerning what to do when turning at intersections of multi-lane roads, both with and without traffic lights. It is very possible that the student won't have the experience to understand the manual however, so the teacher must clarify the rules.

Chapter Four

···✦✦✦···

Multi-Lane Roads

Driving on multi-lane roads means higher speeds and lane changes. The motions and steps to accomplish a lane change should be practiced in a safe environment, like a large parking lot, that has a few vehicles in the parking spaces.

The summary of steps to making a safe lane change is: signal, mirror, mirror, blind spot, small turn, turn back.

Explanation

"Signal" is first because it puts other drivers on alert before your action occurs.

"Mirror" means look into the rear view mirror inside the vehicle to check for faster vehicles approaching from behind and for vehicles and motorcycles darting through traffic. They could make sudden moves that put them alongside the vehicle as the lane change begins.

"Mirror" the second time means look into the outside mirror that is on the side of the vehicle in the direction the lane change is being made. In other words, when changing to the left, check the left mirror. The point is to make sure there is no other vehicle in the way.

"Blind spot" means check the blind spot, which is the area beside the vehicle that is not visible in the two mirrors already checked. If the vehicle is not equipped with blind spot mirrors, the driver will need to look over the shoulder toward the rear fender (left for lane changes to the left and right for lane changes to the right) to attempt to see any vehicles in the way. The movement must be quick to avoid accidentally turning the steering wheel when turning the head. If the vehicle does have blind spot mirrors, the driver can check for other vehicles in the blind spot without looking backward while driving forward. It's especially good for those with issues in turning the head. The owner's manuals of vehicles equipped with lane change warnings call that feature an "aid" and tell the owner not to rely on it. The lane change warning features do not give sufficient warning time when there is a big speed differential between the overtaking vehicle and the vehicle being overtaken. There is also the relative angle of the vehicles to consider. At a yield intersection, the sensors of the turning vehicle may not pick up the crossing traffic in time.

"Small turn" describes how much the steering wheel needs to be turned while making a typical lane change. At about 40 mph or 45 mph, the wheel needs only about 10 degrees of turn to make a smooth lane change, and the turn should not be abrupt.

"Turn back" describes turning the steering wheel in the opposite direction to align with the new lane. This should also be a small turn and smooth.

To practice the lane changes before going on the road, have the student let the vehicle idle forward in drive (or first gear of a manual shift vehicle) and repeatedly go through the motions of a lane change. It helps if the teacher "chants" the steps. The small turns will have little sideways effect on the vehicle at such low speeds but don't let the student hold the turns for a longer time than it would take for a real lane change. The point of the practice is to rehearse the actual motions. When the motions are familiar, more attention is available to judge the safety of the lane change.

It may take the student five or ten practice lane changes to get the pattern down.

When the student has the lane change motions down pat, direct the student to park near another parked vehicle in such a way as to put the other vehicle in the blind spot. That convinces the student that a blind spot really exists. While s/he may partially see a large SUV, the student will appreciate that a sub compact vehicle, a small sports car, or a motorcycle would not be seen.

Next, have the student move forward a couple of vehicle lengths and stop. Have the student look over the shoulder as well as into the blind spot and side mirrors to see what, "too close to make a lane change" looks like.

Note

The vehicle used by the student may not have blind spot mirrors, so checking the appearance of a safe or unsafe distance over the shoulder is wiser than other methods.

Then move farther forward and stop to show the student what the picture in the mirrors and over the shoulder look like when there is a safe enough distance for a lane change.

To practice the lane changes, proceed to a multi-lane road with a speed limit in the 40 mph or 45 mph range and experiencing light traffic.

Note

Make sure there is plenty of safe distance for the first few lane changes. It is best to make the changes on the sections of road that are straight since the student will be looking away from the road. You will need to tell the student to maintain speed during the lane changes. The beginner tends to lift the foot off the accelerator when starting lane changes. A slight increase in speed would not be out of line since the lane change requires moving sideways and thus reducing the forward motion. Make as many lane changes as needed to get the student into the rhythm of changing lanes. Once the student has the rhythm and doesn't need to think about the steps, the student will be more careful at gauging distances.

This is also the time to accent the need to look more in the rear-view mirror since the student doesn't need to place as much attention on the driving skills.

On four-lane roads there is no requirement to stay in one lane or another. The teacher should give lane change directions that 1) practice safe distance lane changing, 2) demonstrate how reading traffic to understand what other drivers are doing can make the student's drive better.

Explanation

As the student's lane changes become more automatic, the student will have time to think about what is going on around him/her. The teacher can point out traffic situations like: a) A large truck ahead in the same lane will be slow leaving the next traffic light so now would be the time to change to a different lane; b) A turn to the right is going to be the next direction change but the right lane is beginning to have close traffic all the way to the turn. That means now is the best time to get into the desired lane. c) The vehicle ahead is tailgating the vehicle in front of it, so the student should leave extra space between vehicles because the two in front are more likely to crash; d) Sometimes the teacher can foresee that a nearby vehicle is going to need to take an action but hasn't done so yet. The teacher should predict that expected move to the student to demonstrate that the student should also anticipate what other drivers may do. e) Other drivers often visibly prepare for changes by looking in the rear view mirror, slowing, or moving to one side of their lane and that may be the only signal they give. f) Keep up to date with traffic that is behind and note where there are gaps as well as where the other vehicles are.

Vehicles joining the road at intersections or from turn lanes may appear to be on a collision course that worries the student. Point out to the student that watching the direction of the front wheel of the other vehicle shows where it is headed. The student should expect the other vehicle's wheel to straighten when it gets to the first open lane.

Slowing and stopping at the higher speeds requires practical experience in eyeballing how much room to leave, so practice both slowing to make a turn to a new road and to stop for traffic lights.

Practice at least one turn to the left and one turn to the right. More would be better.

Explanation

Many four-lane roads have lanes intended to be used for slowing and turning off the four-lane road. Tell the student that the turn lanes are where most of the slowing for turns should be done. The student should not do much, or any, slowing in the travel lanes if possible. That will reduce the opportunity of being rear-ended.

Practice stopping.

Note

Stopping for a traffic light can be more complicated to a student than it sounds. If the distance to stop is ordinary or long, the student should put the foot on the brake early, but lightly, just enough to light the brake lights, which will warn any driver behind that the student is going to stop – not run the yellow light.

If the distance is short and stronger than normal braking is begun, the student needs to look in the rear-view mirror to see if any vehicle behind can also stop in time. If the vehicle behind cannot stop in time, the student must consider evasive actions or prepare for impact. Possible actions are: (1) lane change if there's time and room; (2) move closer to the vehicle ahead to give more room to the vehicle behind; (3) run the red light if the head of the line of crossing traffic is stopped.

This may be a good time to make a practice U-turn if traffic and the road permit.

Review state laws with the student about "moving over" and what to do if an emergency vehicle with flashing lights is approaching.

Explanation

Most state laws require a driver approaching police activity or emergency lighted vehicles, like tow trucks and ambulances, to move over one lane or slow significantly if moving over is not safe or possible.

The general requirement for emergency vehicles is for the driver to move to the right to make room for the emergency vehicle, but that doesn't meet every situation.

If the lesson is going well, consider changing to a road with higher speeds, perhaps one with a 55 mph or 60 mph speed limit. The closer to interstate speeds that the student gets to drive, the less intimidated the student will be at the thought of driving on the interstate roads.

If the lesson is not going well, it's time to assess whether the student is capable of becoming a driver.

Explanation

Safe driving requires that the driver constantly take in sights and sounds, judge their importance, and react appropriately to the stimuli in conjunction with completing the driver's plan. In addition, the driver must be aware of the route being traveled, where s/he is, what the speed limit is, which lane to be in for the next turn, and other traffic. For some people, that is too much information to consider or prioritize. If you find yourself doubting the capability of the student at this point, it's probably not the first time you have had doubts.

Driving on multi-lane roads is the most complicated part of driving in terms of how many things to keep in mind at the same time, and it is only topped by higher speed multi-lane roads and interstate driving, which will be the next level. Correct responses will need to be done faster. The length of time a student can pay attention to everything is another factor.

Those people diagnosed as having behavior in the autism spectrum, with attention deficit, or with metabolic disorders can become drivers if the effects are not too significant and if medication is taken responsibly. It would be cruel, however, to lead someone on who couldn't control impulses or physical actions to the degree of being unsafe, even if they could pass the road test.

Chapter Five

···✦◆✦···

Interstate Driving

Driving on the interstates requires more planning than driving on ordinary multi-lane roads. An ideal time to introduce the student to the interstate is near the end of a successful lesson on multi-lane roads at relatively high speed. The student in that case will be "warmed up" on lane changes and speed, and the first experience on the interstate will necessarily, because of time constraints, be short. New drivers are anxious the first time on interstates. You can plan on the student being stressed, so don't announce your plan until it's time.

The plan should include considering where to enter the interstate.

Success is more likely if the teacher demonstrates the merge maneuver, travels a short distance to an exit, demonstrates the exit maneuver and then tells the student to do the same actions.

Explanation

If possible, the first time the student drives on the interstate should be on a part of the system with a speed limit close to the speed the student has driven before, and with traffic that is moderate or light.

The student will be less tense if not worried about a new speed. The entrance ramp chosen for the student's first trip should be one that allows plenty of room both for the acceleration to highway speed and for merging into traffic, and it should also have good sightlines to the traffic flow.

Traffic flow on the interstate is already moving at a higher speed than the student has likely driven. To safely join that flow, the student should accelerate on the entrance ramp to be at the interstate speed at the time of merging into the traffic flow. Try to avoid getting on the ramp with a noticeably slow vehicle ahead.

Problem: You see a clearly slow vehicle ahead on the entrance ramp which will prevent the student from merging at the interstate speed.

Solution: Have the student stay well back and allow distance to build up between the slow vehicle and the student's vehicle. That leaves space for the student to accelerate to highway speeds even if the slow vehicle doesn't. It may mean that the student will need to make an immediate lane change to avoid the slow vehicle after the merge. It could also mean braking after the merge if there is no space in the next lane.

Tell the student to merge as soon as safely possible and not run to the end of the acceleration lane.

Explanation

A merge is like a lane change except there is no need to look directly behind. Some entrance ramps are positioned in a way that allows a driver who is entering the interstate to see the traffic early, select a gap to fit into, and adjust speed to arrive at the same time as the gap. Other entrance ramps don't allow such early positioning. The process in both cases is to accelerate to the interstate speed, signal, look at the side mirror and at the blind spot for a gap to move into, make a small turn into the new lane, straighten the vehicle in the lane, and adjust speed to match the traffic.

Keys to safe interstate driving include staying in lane, leaving enough following distance for the new speeds, planning ahead for lane changes, maintaining steady speed, acting in a predictable manner, and planning in advance to be in the correct lane for exits.

Note

Reading traffic is important to lane planning and to avoiding "hurry up" lane changes. For instance, in a case where the driver notices a hill a half mile or mile ahead, and the driver also notices a large tractor trailer between his vehicle and the hill, the driver who is paying attention understands that the truck is likely to slow on the hill, causing a traffic backup. The thoughtful driver, at that point, will plan and make a lane change to the left early to avoid both the slow truck and the traffic behind it.

Thoughtful planning also comes into play when changing from one interstate system to another. Tractor trailers often slow at such exits if the drivers aren't sure what will be a safe speed for the ramp. The slowing trucks can cause traffic congestion a mile back from an exit if traffic is heavy. The thoughtful driver will change to the exit lane early just to be sure s/he can make the exit as planned without causing someone else to have an emergency.

If the student driver comes upon one tractor trailer passing another, the student driver following the passing vehicle should expect the tractor trailer driver to signal a move to the right at the point when the student's vehicle is about even with the front of the tractor trailer being passed. The student should not jump in front of the truck being passed and then pass the first truck on the right. The student should wait for the passing truck to move back to the right.

When taking a trip, the route should be thought out beforehand so the driver knows in advance which exit to take and which direction to turn. Software programs and apps used to give directions may not be current with road construction or other detours, and crashes may cause short term changes as well. It is a good idea to know the major highways used as alternates to the interstates.

Much of the driving on an interstate can be uneventful. That is a good time to bring up how interstates are numbered, their relationship to U. S. routes, as well as the value of mile markers and their use.

Explanation

Interstate highways that run primarily north/south are odd numbered roads, just like the U. S. routes. Interstate highways that run east/west are even numbered. State roads, county roads, etc., follow the same pattern.

There are two ways that interstate exits are numbered. One way is the sequential method. The exits are numbered in the order they occur. The first is exit one, the second is exit two no matter how far apart they are, and so on.

The other way interstate exits are numbered is by mile they are in. So exit 114 is in mile 114. The advantage of this method to the driver is s/he can calculate the distance to the planned exit from the mile markers. The advantage to a transportation department is there is no need to change the signage if a new exit is added.

Most interstate highways between cities are built along the same path as a U.S. route. One east coast example is Interstate 95 which parallels U.S. Route One. In the event of a crash or other blockage on I95, traffic can be moved to the U. S. route to detour around the blockage and proceed ahead to the next interstate entrance.

Interstate highways have mile markers placed along the side of the highways at regular intervals and on bridges and overpasses. If there is a crash or a breakdown, reporting the mile marker nearest to where it occurred can give more precise location information to emergency services.

Periodically tell the student to check the speedometer and drive his/her own speed.

Explanation

> There is a natural proclivity for a driver to match the speed of passing vehicles and to maintain a constant distance to other vehicles. It is a mistake to let other drivers determine the student's speed. Tell the student what is happening so the student can monitor him/herself.

Discuss drowsiness with the student.

Explanation

> A new driver has not experienced becoming drowsy behind the wheel and needs to be warned to take steps to keep alert. The first sign of drowsiness is usually yawning. Counteracting drowsiness is important to mention because interstate driving can be monotonous and lead to drowsiness. It isn't good enough to say "Get off at the next exit." There is often a significant distance to travel to the next interstate exit so the new driver needs tactics to stay awake until s/he can take a break from driving.

Ways to combat drowsiness

> The basic strategies for combating drowsiness include activity and extra stimuli. So try bouncing in the seat, pushing a foot against the floor (not accelerator) really hard, squeezing both hands toward the middle of the

steering wheel, pushing down on the steering wheel, listening to fast and loud music, opening a window, turning on the air conditioner in winter, turning on the heat in the summer, singing, talking, or biting your lip.

When planning to leave the interstate, tell the student to move into the correct lane early enough to smoothly make the exit. Tell the student to maintain interstate speed until on the exit ramp (traffic permitting).

Explanation

Slowing for the exit would create an "accordion" effect on the traffic behind the exiting vehicle and raise the likelihood of a crash, including a rear-ending of the student's vehicle. The student also should be warned that other drivers commonly slow to exit, so the student should leave extra room between vehicles near the exit points.

Tell the student that stopping from 70 mph requires much more distance than expected.

Explanation

Hard or emergency stopping from 70 mph (using ABS activating levels of pressure on the brake) will take about 175 feet for ordinary passenger vehicles. That distance is about the typical distance between utility poles along a two-lane roadway.

Tell the student, who just exited the interstate to drive again on local roads, to check his/her speed on the speedometer.

Explanation

> Switching from driving on the interstate to driving on local roads at an exit brings with it a need to adjust to slower speeds. After driving at interstate speeds for a while, any lower speed seems slow but, in fact, the driver may be driving faster than believed. The just-ended high speed travel conditions the driver's perception, a phenomenon called "velocitation." It is defined as a psychological tendency to be traveling at a speed that is faster than perceived. So as a practical matter, the driver who exited the 70-mph interstate feels s/he is driving very slowly but the vehicle actual speed might be 50 mph in a 35-mph zone. The driver needs to mentally reorient to the new speed limits by checking against the speedometer when first leaving the interstate.

The teacher will need to schedule a number of on/off evolutions on the interstate in the next lesson to give the student enough confidence not to be a hazard to other drivers at interstate entrances and exits. The reason for that is a student lacking confidence hesitates and commits unpredictable actions.

Chapter Six

...✦✦✦...

Emergency Lane Change

Beginning drivers are more likely to get into emergencies because they don't have the experience to recognize when an emergency is developing. Emergency level stopping was practiced in the first or second lesson to give the student confidence by knowing how quickly s/he could stop a vehicle. However, sometimes stopping isn't the best solution. Sometimes it is best to avoid a serious problem by braking and turning into a different lane in a very fast fashion.

When the teacher has set the exercise up according to the arrangement on pages 80-82, the teacher should give the student scenarios to explain when to use the procedure.

Here's one scenario: two vehicles in front of the student's vehicle crash and perhaps the student could stop in time but a tractor trailer behind the student might not. Another scenario would be that a large piece of metal falls from a truck into the student's lane. Perhaps the student could stop in time, but the driver behind the student won't see the metal until the student is out of the way, and merely stopping will cause the student to be rear-ended. In either of the two scenarios above, the student may not be able to stop in time to avoid the crash – only slow.

The teacher should do a slow run through to demonstrate the actions to take and emphasize the importance of the student calling the direction to go, which starts the emergency. The emergency starts for the teacher when the front of the vehicle is about even with the indicator cone and the student shouts the direction to take (either LEFT or RIGHT).

The actions to make an emergency lane change are; when the emergency starts, the driver brakes firmly, looks where to go, turns into another lane (or onto a shoulder of the road), then straightens the vehicle to remain in the new lane. Those actions keep the driver from joining the problem or being shoved into it by a vehicle from behind.

It's important that the teacher steer sharply, more that a swerve, in avoiding the obstacles. A swerve may work at slow speeds but at higher speeds on the road, the swerve technique will either not be enough to avoid a crash or could result in running off the road.

Add to the speed over several repetitions so that it is clear that vigorous action is appropriate. Then the teacher calls the direction for the student to react. Start the student with a few slow runs so the student can learn the motions. Next, have the student increase the speed. The arrangement of the exercise should allow for a 25 – 30 mph run. It isn't important that the student reach the exercise maximum. It's enough that the student approaches his/her limit with the knowledge s/he can accomplish the maneuver.

Emergency Lane Change Exercise

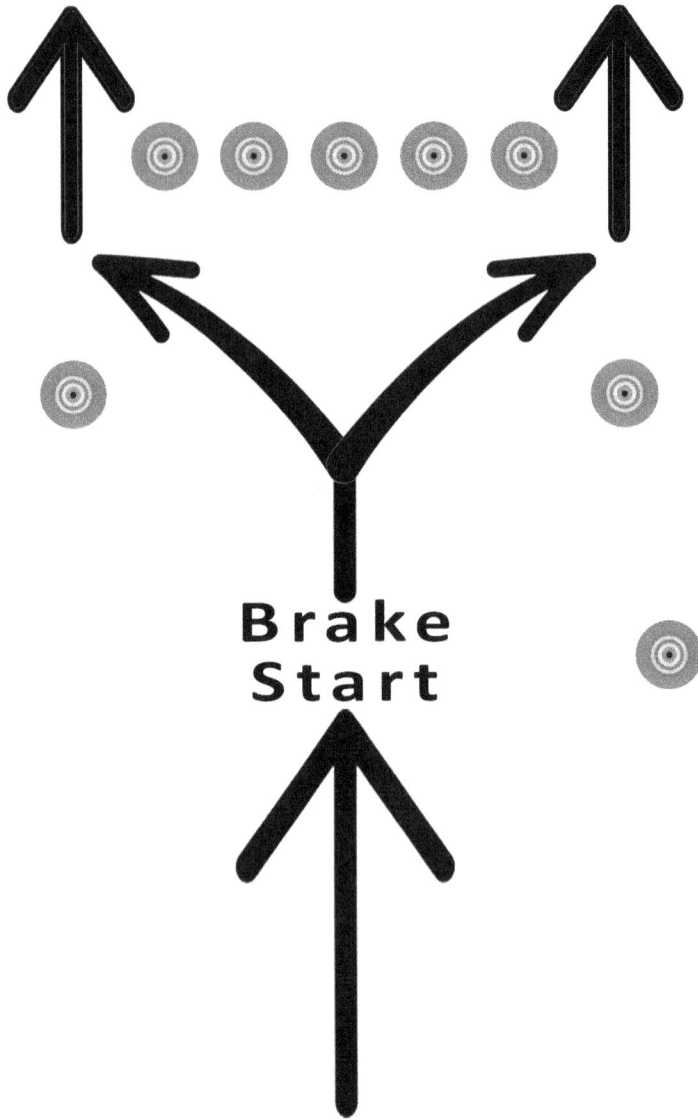

Brake
Start

= cone, box, etc.

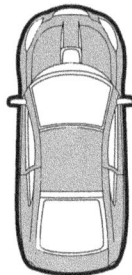

How to Teach Driving
by Kenneth Lindquist

The five obstacles (cones, milk containers, or boxes) aligned perpendicular to the exercise line of travel, represent an emergency situation that hasn't happened yet. They are placed one side-step apart to approximate the width of a passenger vehicle.

Two more obstacles are placed six paces closer to the vehicle with each of them one sidestep to the outside of the emergency obstacles. They are pivot obstacles.

One last obstacle is placed seven paces closer toward the vehicle and one sidestep to the right of the rightmost of the pivot obstacles. That is the cue obstacle.

Operation of the exercise

The vehicle proceeds toward the five obstacles. As the front of the vehicle nears the cue obstacle, the person sitting in the passenger seat shouts "left" or "right". That shout is the start of the emergency. The driver then must brake (but not stop), release the brake, look where to go, and turn in the direction that was shouted, drive between the pivot obstacle and the emergency obstacles. Then quickly turn back in the original direction of travel. The effect is an emergency lane change to another lane or road shoulder which will keep the vehicle out of the emergency but stay on pavement.

The purpose of braking is to lessen any collision and to shift more of the vehicle's weight onto the front tires. Releasing the brake immediately as turning starts leaves more traction for turning. Higher weight on the front tires gives the vehicle the ability to turn without sliding at a speed 10-15% faster than not braking.

Vigorous steering is needed to accomplish the movements at the higher end of the speed range possible in the exercise. Simply swerving is not sufficient because it can take the vehicle off the pavement or farther than one lane.

Chapter Seven

·•·✦·✦·✦··

Road Test

It is a good idea to practice the road test before taking the state exam. A nervous student driver clenches when facing the road test, so easing the tension by going over the course will help the student driver be tested on driving skills instead of on adrenaline level. The teacher could follow other students being tested, at a respectful distance of course, to find out the routes used for the license examination, and practice with the student when the road test center is closed.

In some states, high schools can issue waivers of road tests for teens based on driver education coursework. However, the confidence gained from passing a road test will be helpful when the student makes that first drive alone.

… AND BEYOND

After about 6 months of driving by themselves, teen drivers begin to rely on their "vast" experience instead of what they were taught, and they start taking driving shortcuts. It is a good time for parents to conduct their own road test and/or send the new driver to an advanced course. Many car clubs (Mercedes, BMW, Porsche, Sports

Car Club of America, Tire Rack, Ford Motor Co.) offer courses in wreck avoidance and you don't need to be a member. There are commercial racing schools that offer teen/new driver advanced training. Some schools specialize in driving on snow.

Chapter Eight

∙∙∙✦✦✦∙∙∙

Driving at Night

Begin by planning to take the student driving at night on a lightly used road that the student is familiar with. A half hour should be a long enough introduction at the simple traffic level.

Explanation

> There are fewer visual cues when driving in the dark so it is easier for the student to miss a usual turn-in point at an intersection or misjudge when to start braking for a stop. Starting on a familiar road will minimize the magnitude of the misses.

Go over the settings on the light switch and adjust the brightness of the dashboard lights before starting.

Explanation

> Make sure the night driving lights are the ones being used. Some vehicles use low-powered headlights as daytime driving lights and drivers can be fooled into thinking their headlights are on when instead, it's the

low-powered lights too weak to use at night. With some vehicles, the daytime light setting does not light the taillights and that would be dangerous at night.

The student probably doesn't know that the dashboard lights are adjustable or where the adjustment is made. The brightness level needed for day is much higher than that needed for night and, to the student, the daylight level might be distracting or affect night vision.

Have the student practice changing from low beam to high beam and back. It can be done while keeping the hands on the steering wheel. Point out the indicator of high beam on the dashboard.

Tell the student to shut the lights off and then tell the student to flash the high beams to show that the lights can be flashed even if they aren't turned on.

Advise the student not to look at the oncoming lights. Instead, the student should look to the right edge of the road a bit farther than the reach of the lights. The student should be watching for human feet, bicycles, and large animals.

Tell the student to use high beams as much as is possible without blinding other drivers. The state rules will prescribe the distance at which high beams must be switched to low beams.

When driving behind another vehicle and using low beam lights, the student should be looking ahead at what is illuminated by the lights of the vehicle in front of him/her.

Explanation

The lights of the vehicle in front will illuminate pedestrians, bicycles, and large animals earlier than the student's own lights and any obstacles between the front vehicle and the student's vehicle will be shown in profile. If the vehicle in front makes sudden moves, it may be that the driver ahead sees a pothole or bit of rough road. In that way the following driver, the student, is warned by watching traffic ahead.

Tell the student to be aware of the look of traffic in the rear-view mirrors while traveling on the lightly used road.

Explanation

Judging how far away a vehicle is by the size or intensity of the headlights requires some practice. If the student wears glasses, there will be a period of adjustment. Extra reflections will appear in the glasses unless the glasses have an anti-glare coating.

The student may not be aware that the rear-view mirror inside the vehicle has a dimmer setting that the student can use if the headlights behind the student are too bright and causing distraction. However, it does make judging distance more difficult when comparing the appearances of vehicle lights in the rear-view mirror to that of the appearances in the side mirrors.

The student may feel a vehicle behind is deliberately using high beams as a harassment when actually what is happening is the vehicle behind is higher or taller and because of that even the low beams shine more directly into the student's vehicle.

Next, direct the student to a multi-lane road or interstate and point out the differences between low traffic volume, single lane roads, and the higher use highways.

Explanation

There are more things to see, just as in daylight, but it is harder to interpret them from the fewer cues.

If the student is overtaking a vehicle with an odd appearance to the lights (it could be a trailer, a farm vehicle, a motorcycle with a sidecar, etc.), s/he needs to overtake more slowly until the reason for the unusual appearance is clear and appropriate action can be taken.

The student needs to wait slightly before making a lane change if another vehicle is overtaking him/her. The passing vehicle could be pulling a trailer that isn't visible until it's alongside.

Properly adjusted high beams shine just far enough ahead to see and avoid objects in the road at about 70 mph. Overdriving your lights means you are driving too fast to see and avoid objects ahead.

In city traffic, the student can check to see if his/her taillights and brake lights are working by looking at the reflections of those lights on the front of the vehicle behind them at traffic stops.

Review using the lights to signal acknowledgement of a truck's turn signal, and how to flash a warning to another driver.

Explanation

If a truck driver on a multi-lane road puts on a signal to turn into the student's lane, it should be interpreted as the truck driver asking for room to move over in front of the driver. If the driver is going to make room for the truck or agrees to leave the current space open, the driver should flash the lights once or twice to let the truck driver know he can safely move over.

If a vehicle approaching from the front is heading toward stopped traffic he can't see, or a crash, or some other problem, the driver can flash the lights twice or several groups of 2 flashes to warn the oncoming driver of danger.

Chapter Nine

...•••◆•••...

Problem Diagnosis and Solutions

Steering and Turning

Lane management problems at slow speed

Symptom: Wandering from one side of the lane to the other even though looking ahead.

> **Cause:** (1) Steering inputs too large.
> **Solution:** Practice part of one lesson in a cemetery or a similar location where the roads are one-way and narrow to accustom the student to less movement.

> **Cause:** (2) One hand higher on the steering wheel than the other.
> **Solution:** Instruct the student to keep his/her hands at the same height on the steering wheel when driving straight.

Typical turning mistakes and their solutions

Symptom: Slowing too much in turns.

> **Cause:** Nervousness, lack of experience, and lack of confidence.
>
> **Solution:** Practice is the answer to all the causes. The experienced driver turns at about 12 mph. Concentrate on a steady speed during the turn. The student's turning speed will increase naturally.

Symptom: Hitting the curb with the rear wheel on right turns.

> **Cause:** (1) Turns too soon.
>
> **Solution:** Start to turn when the curb or corner disappears from view in the right corner of the windshield.

> **Cause:** (2) Starts the turn with the vehicle too close to the curb.
>
> **Solution:** The turn can be done better by starting from the center of the lane.

Symptom: Crossing the center line of the new road in right turn, making a big turn to the right and a big turn to the left.

> **Cause:** (1) Starts the turn too close to the curb.
>
> **Solution:** The turn can be done better by starting from the center of the lane.

> **Cause:** (2) Delays the quarter-turn-motion part of the turn.

Solution: Explain to the student that the turning motion is a one-two action. First comes the half turn with both hands on the wheel and then the right grabs the wheel at the 12 o'clock position and pulls the wheel down. There is no pause in the one-two.

Cause: (3) The student might be looking at the center line instead of the lane.

Solution: Remind the student that the car will go where the driver is looking so the driver should look at the lane of the new road.

Cause (4) Pulling the vehicle close to the crossing street to see any oncoming traffic made the turn very tight.

Solution: For a very tight right turn, tell the student to start turning the wheel <u>before</u> applying the gas.

Symptom: Taking too long to get speed back up after a turn.

Cause: Thinking about the just completed turn.

Solution: Remind the student to increase speed back to the travel speed as soon as the turn is completed. Explain that the others using the road and catching up behind are already traveling at that speed.

Symptom: Straightening the steering wheel too soon coming out of a turn.

Cause: Lack of experience and a worry that a lot of hand speed is needed to turn the steering wheel in time.

Solution: Assure the student that waiting until the vehicle is headed straight in the driving lane will leave enough time to straighten the steering wheel.

Symptom: Overshooting the proper lane on turns.

Cause: Putting the hand inside the steering wheel, palm up, while turning.

Solution: Remind the student to keep the hands on the outside of the steering wheel. There are three reasons to do so: 3. The palm up hand position is very restrictive, allowing only about a quarter turn of the wheel; 2. The forearm is situated over the air bag with the fingers looped around the wheel, potentially causing a very painful extension of the fingers if the air bag explodes; 1. The most important reason is the driver's eyes are looking inside the vehicle to avoid hitting the steering wheel spokes with the hand while the driver is turning.

Lane keeping Problems

Symptom: Moving the wheel too much, sawing back and forth.

Cause: (1) If the movement is constant, the student is looking right in front of the vehicle.

Solution: Tell the student to look farther ahead.

Cause: (2) If the movement is two moves, one in each direction with a pause in between, then two moves again, the student is steering too much on the first input and then correcting it.

Solution: Tell the student that as the vehicle speed increases, the steering inputs need to be smaller.

Symptom; Steering from one side of the lane to the other, like zigzagging, or tacking.

Cause: Alternating between looking at the left then right edges of the lane instead of the center of the lane.

Solution: Tell the student to look farther ahead at the center of the lane.

Symptom; Hugging one side of the lane or the other.

Cause: The student may fear oncoming traffic or running off the road.

Solution: If the student stays on the right side of the lane, let the student know how much room there is to the left by telling the student to steer the left side wheels over the yellow "Bott's dots" (small reflectors) in the yellow paint separating the opposing traffic flows. The student will be very surprised at how much room is available. If the student stays to the left side of the lane, tell the student to drive over something to the right. There may be "dots" or rumble strips, or you could direct the student to deliberately run off the edge of the road (in a safe place, of course). Tell the student to choose reference points on the vehicle like the end of a wiper blade, a windshield washer nozzle, or other features to use as reference points to estimate where the wheels are going to travel.

Braking

Symptom: Braking hard for traffic stops.

> **<u>Cause:</u>** (1) Doesn't know how to make a gentle stop.
>
> **<u>Solution:</u>** A gentle stop can be reached by slowing almost to a stop then easing the foot pressure off the brake so that the full stop comes while moving 1 or 2 mph instead of from 10 mph.
>
> **<u>Cause:</u>** (2) Braking too late for smooth, steady deceleration.
>
> **<u>Solution:</u>** Practice braking sooner.
>
> **<u>Cause:</u>** (3) Abrupt braking on all stops.
>
> **<u>Solution:</u>** Keep the heel on the floor and modulate the brake pedal with the calf muscle for ordinary stops.

Accelerating

Symptom: Accelerating and changing speed abruptly.

> **<u>Cause:</u>** Using leg muscles to control the gas pedal.
>
> **<u>Solution:</u>** (1) Keep the right heel on the floor and control the accelerator with the calf muscles.
>
> **<u>Solution:</u>** (2) Don't try to drive while wearing high heeled shoes.

About Kenneth Lindquist

Kenneth Lindquist is a driving instructor, amateur sports-car racer, teen driving-clinic instructor, and the parent designated to teach three daughters. He is a member of the Sports Car Club of America (SCCA) and the American Driver and Traffic Safety Education Association (ADTSEA). Founder of the Red Mountain Driving Academy, Ken lives near Birmingham, Alabama.

Fresh Ink Group

Independent Multi-media Publisher

Fresh Ink Group / Voice of Indie / GeezWriter / Push Pull Press

&

Hardcovers
Softcovers
All Ebook Formats
Audiobooks
Podcasts
Worldwide Distribution

&

Indie Author Services
Book Development, Editing, Proofing
Graphic/Cover Design
Video/Trailer Production
Website Creation
Social Media Marketing
Writing Contests
Writers' Blogs

&

Authors
Editors
Artists
Experts
Professionals

&

FreshInkGroup.com
info@FreshInkGroup.com
Twitter: @FreshInkGroup
Facebook.com/FreshInkGroup
LinkedIn: Fresh Ink Group

Fresh Ink Group
FreshInkGroup.com

How to Teach Driving
Behind the Wheel, Lesson by Lesson
Instructors' Edition

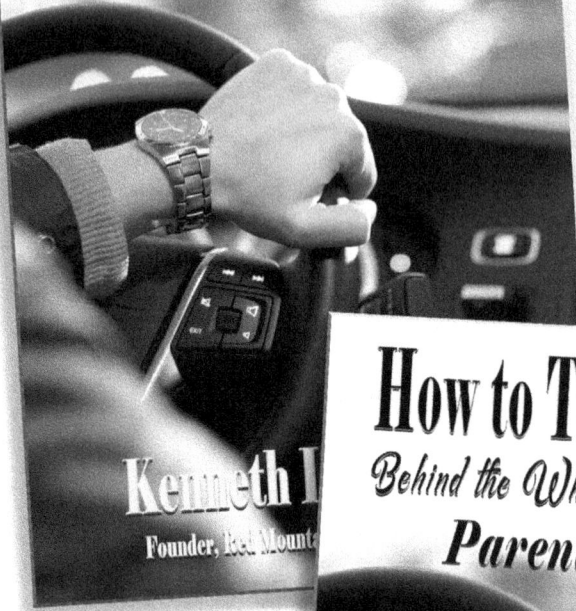

Kenneth L...
Founder, Red Mounta...

Time
to
Learn

Time
to
Teach

How to Teach Driving
Behind the Wheel, Lesson by Lesson
Parents' Edition

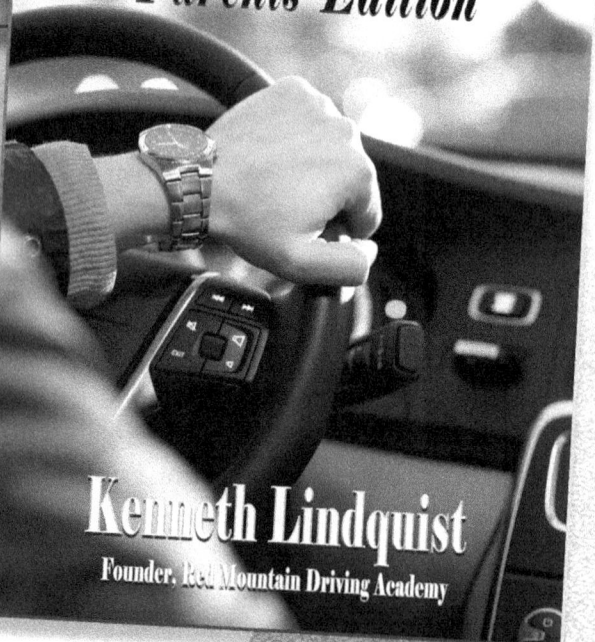

Kenneth Lindquist
Founder, Red Mountain Driving Academy

Fresh Ink Group
FreshInkGroup.com

How to Start and Run Your Own Food Truck Business In Florida

FOOD TRUCK

A. K. Wingler

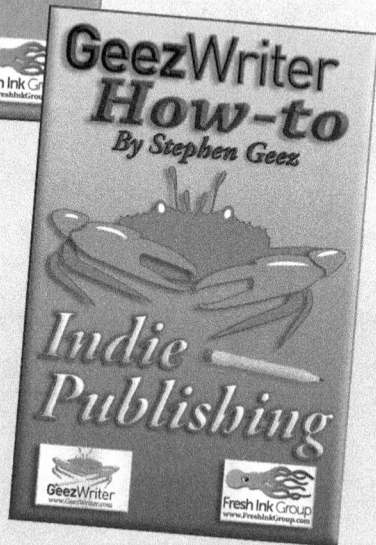

Fresh Ink Group

Short Story Showcase #1

Edited by
Stephen Geez

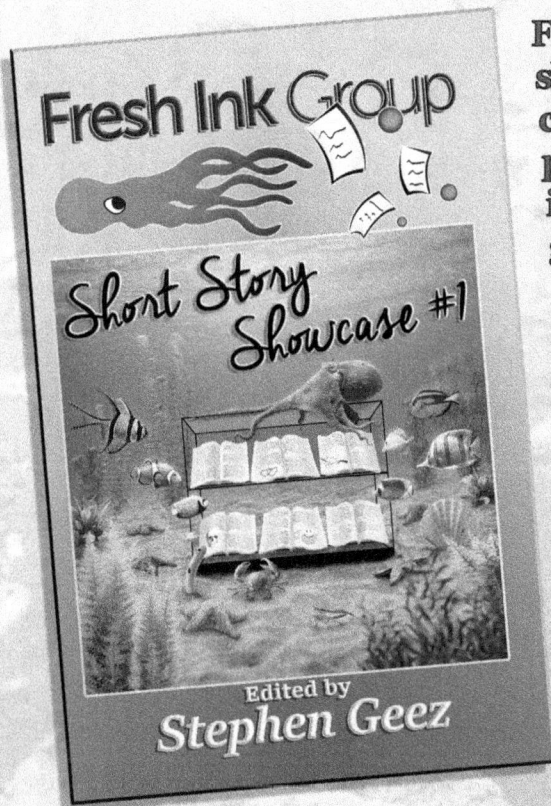

Fresh Ink Group showcases 42 compelling prize-winners from its literary and genre short-story contests. Eclectic, daring, subtle, provocative, diverse—this wide-ranging collection by authors from across the USA and around the world transcends the limits of single-theme anthologies to explore the best of many styles and bold new ideas. Travel through time and space. Experience the Dust Bowl, a dying soldier's love, one distraught boy's mirror, the southern-farm snake, suicidal love lost, politicians run amok, a serial killer's lair, seductive sorcerous charms, a malevolent-house warning, inevitable moon-base death, the vengeful walking corpse, or a Holocaust child's hope, the lament of a life never lived . . . Discerning story-lovers are invited to listen for the voices of these newly favorite authors in Fresh Ink Group Short Story Showcase #1. Keep turning the pages to discover what unexpected delights beckon next.

www.ingramcontent.com/pod-product-compliance
Lightning Source LLC
LaVergne TN
LVHW081324060426
835511LV00011B/1838